EASY CARD TRICKS

Stephanie Turnbull

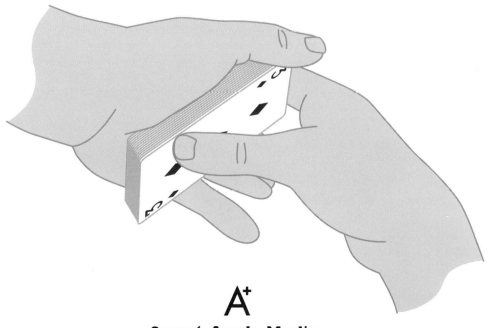

A+

Smart Apple Media

Published by Smart Apple Media, an imprint of Black Rabbit Books
P.O. Box 3263, Mankato, Minnesota, 56002
www.blackrabbitbooks.com

Printed in the United States of America, at Corporate Graphics
in North Mankato, Minnesota.

Designed and illustrated by Guy Callaby
Edited by Mary-Jane Wilkins

Library of Congress Cataloging-in-Publication Data

Turnbull, Stephanie.
  Easy Card tricks / Stephanie Turnbull.
     pages cm. -- (Beginner magic)
  Includes index.
  ISBN 978-1-62588-006-2 (library bound)
  1. Card tricks--Juvenile literature. I. Title.
  GV1549.T85 2014
  793.8'5--dc23

                            2012051807

Photo acknowledgements
page 2 iStockphoto/Thinkstock;
4 Hemera/Thinkstock, 5 eAlisa/Shutterstock
Front cover: Getty Images/Thinkstock,
iStockphoto/Thinkstock

DAD0508
052013
9 8 7 6 5 4 3 2 1

Contents

Do you want to amaze your friends with card tricks? All you need is this book, a pack of cards and some practice.

Know your cards

There should be 52 cards in your pack, divided into four suits: hearts, diamonds, spades and clubs. You don't need the jokers, so take them out. Try not to bend or crease cards, as it may ruin tricks.

Hearts

Diamonds

Spades

Clubs

The front of a card is the face. When it is showing, the card is face up. When the back is showing, the card is face down. All the backs look the same so you can't tell them apart.

Back

Tips and Ideas

Look out for these boxes as you read this book. They're full of handy tips for making tricks work perfectly.

Magic Secrets

You can also discover secrets of master magicians in these boxes... but don't tell anyone!

Playing cards have existed for hundreds of years.

Quick Card Tidy Up

Here's an easy trick to get you started. It helps you practice dealing, which means laying out cards on the table.

1. Find all the cards from one suit and lay them out from lowest to highest: ace (1), 2, 3, 4, 5, 6, 7, 8, 9, 10, jack, queen, king. Show a friend.

2. Now put the cards in a pile, keeping them in order. Hold them face down.

3. Tell your friend you'll deal them into a new pile and they must help mix them by calling **"One"** or **"Two"**.

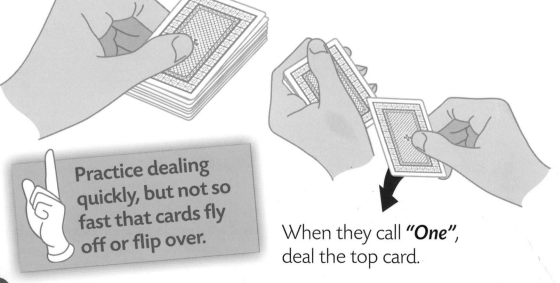

Practice dealing quickly, but not so fast that cards fly off or flip over.

When they call **"One"**, deal the top card.

When they call **"Two"**, slide the top card under the next card...

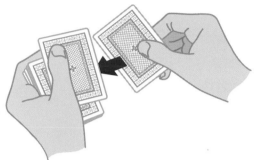

...then put down the two cards together.

4. When you've dealt all the cards, pick up the pile and do it all again, so your friend can mix them even more.

5. Now say you'll tidy the cards with magic! Snap your fingers or say magic words, then turn over the pile and spread out the cards. They're back in the right order!

This trick works because switching the cards doesn't mix them. Try it with the cards face up to check.

Amazing Mind-Reader

This neat trick involves cutting, which means moving cards from the top of the pack to the bottom.

1. Ask a friend to mix the pack of cards on the table while you explain that you have mind-reading powers. When they hand you the mixed pack, peek at the bottom card. Remember it!

2. Tell your friend to take the top card, memorize it and put it back.

Magic Secrets

Magicians do lots of acting to make people think they're reading minds.

3. Put down the pack. Cut it by taking a chunk of cards off the top and putting them on the table...

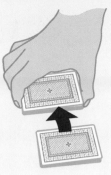

...then placing the rest of the pack on top.

Do this a few times so the cards seem to be mixed. In fact, the order won't change at all.

4. Pretend to read your friend's mind, then fan out the pack and find the card you saw.

Ask your friend to cut the cards, so they know you're not doing anything sneaky!

Your friend's card will always be the next card to the right.

Pull it out and say, *"I think THIS was your card!"*

Here's a longer trick. Try inventing extra details to add to the story.

1. Lay out the aces, kings, queens, and jacks like this. Say, ***"The Ace family did everything together. So did the King family, the Queen family and the Jack family."***

2. *"One day they went to the movies. The Ace family sat along the back row. The Kings took the next row, then the Queens, then the Jacks."* As you talk, lay out the four groups in overlapping rows.

3. *"When the movie began, everyone started to move around."* Make each overlapping group into a pile and turn them face down. Pick up the first pile and put it on top of the second.

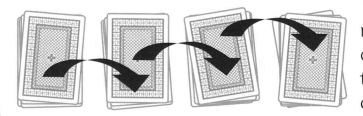

Then pick up the new pile and put it on the third, then the fourth, to create one big pile.

Counting Challenge

Shuffling is the best way to mix cards. It also lets you secretly place certain cards on top!

Why not practice shuffling while watching TV?

1. Hold the pack in your right hand and rest the cards on your left. Lift most of the pack, then drop a few cards in front of those in your left hand...

Hold the pack in your left hand if you're left-handed.

...and a few behind.

Keep going until all the cards are in your left hand. Repeat a few times.

2. After the last shuffle, tilt the cards slightly in your hand and peek at the bottom card. Remember it!

3. Shuffle again, but this time drop the last card, on its own, on TOP of the pack.

Here's your card at the bottom...

... and here it is moving to the top.

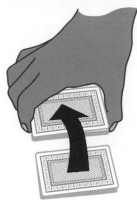

4. *"The families got muddled in the dark. Some went for popcorn and came back; others moved seats."* Cut the cards several times as you speak.

Try cutting cards in your hand. It's quicker than putting them on the table.

5. *"Finally, they rushed out, looking for their families on the way."* Quickly deal the first four cards face down in a line, then the next four on top of each, and so on.

6. *"And would you believe it—all the families were back together!"* As you talk, turn over the piles. The cards are in groups again!

Magic Secrets

Magicians often chat and tell stories so people don't notice what they're doing.

4. Ask your friend to pick a number between one and ten. Say they pick five. Tell them to deal five cards and memorize the fifth. Show them what you mean by dealing five cards face down.

Pick any number between one and ten.

Five.

This is the card you know.

5. Now put the cards you dealt back on TOP of the pack. Let your friend deal five cards. The card they take to memorize is the one you know!

6. Ask them to put their card back in the pack. Give it a few shuffles. Fan out the pack, find your friend's card and pull it out!

THIS is your card!

Magic Secrets
Experts can keep more than one card in place, even though they seem to be shuffling the whole pack.

Calling All Kings

This trick uses a riffle shuffle to keep several cards in place on top of the pack.

Use riffle shuffles in other tricks, too, so it won't look suspicious when you use it here.

1. Beforehand, secretly put the four kings on top of the pack.

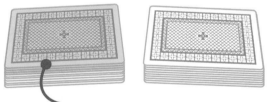

The kings are here.

2. Tell a friend that the kings always appear when you call, even if you don't have the whole pack! As you talk, do a riffle shuffle. First, split the pack in half on a table.

Next, use your thumbs to lift a corner of each half. Move the halves together and let the cards drop down, overlapping as they fall.

Let the last chunk of cards fall on top, so the kings stay in place.

Finally, stand the cards on one long edge and push the halves together. The pack looks mixed, but the kings haven't moved.

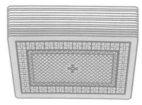

3. Ask your friend to start dealing cards into a pile, face down. Tell them to stop whenever they like, then hide the rest of the pack.

4. Ask them to pick up the dealt pile and deal it into four new piles.

5. Call for the kings, then turn over the top cards. There they are!

This works because the four kings were the last cards your friend dealt.

Magic Secrets

Putting cards in a certain order is called stacking the deck.

Jumping Jacks

The secret of this trick is that you hold more cards than people realize. Practice it well!

Do this trick fairly quickly, so no one gets a long look at the cards you hold.

1. Beforehand, put the four jacks face up in your hand, with three extra cards face down underneath.

These can be any cards.

2. Show a friend that you're holding the jacks, tilting your hand down so they don't see the extra cards. With your other hand, fan out the rest of the pack to prove the jacks are gone.

Magic Secrets

The skill of performing sneaky moves is called sleight of hand.

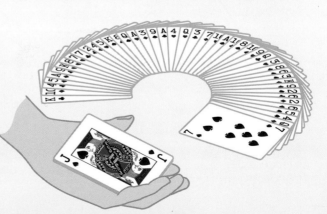

3. Now show each jack by holding them up one at a time, then turning each FACE DOWN and moving it to the back of the pile in your hand.

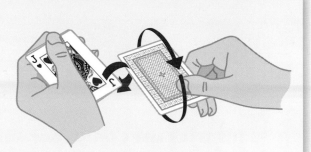

4. Put the pack in a pile face down and put the cards from your hand on top.

5. Say that you will separate the jacks. Take the top card and move it to the bottom of the pack. Slide the next card into the pack just below the middle, and the next card just above the middle.

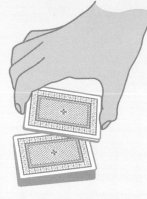

The cards you're moving aren't really jacks, so keep them face down.

6. Say you'll leave the last jack on top. Let everyone see it for a moment.

7. Now say that you can make all the jacks jump up through the pack. Snap your fingers or say magic words, then turn over the top four cards. The jacks are back!

Chase That Ace!

This trick uses only four cards, but needs good memory skills.

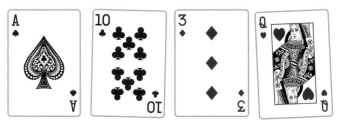

1. Say that you can magically find aces while blindfolded. Ask a friend to choose an ace and three other cards, then lay them out in any order.

Do this each time I shout "Switch!"

2. Tell your friend to swap the ace with either of the cards next to it every time you shout, **"Switch!"** Show them how.

Concentrate on where the ace is —just ignore the other cards.

3. REMEMBER where the ace is in the line, then ask your friend to blindfold you.

The ace is the second card in this line.

4. Shout, *"Switch!",* then again, then three more times, making FIVE switches in total.

Switch!

Switch!

Switch!

Switch!

Switch!

5. If the ace was the first or third card, then it now CAN'T be first in the line. Ask your friend to take away the first card.
If the ace was second or fourth, it now CAN'T be fourth, so ask your friend to remove the fourth card.

Could you pick up the fourth card? Hmm... I can tell it's not the ace. Get rid of that card, please.

6. The ace must now be on the left or right, but you can't tell which. Ask your friend to switch one more time. The ace will be moved to the middle.

7. Ask your friend to remove the third card, then the first... and you're left with the ace.

That must be it!

Magic Fingers

This trick looks complicated at first, but it's easy once you've got the hang of it.

1. Tell a friend that your magical fingers can "sense" cards. As you talk, shuffle the pack, then take a peek at the bottom card. Remember it.

2. Use your fingers to fan the cards on the table, making sure you place your right pinky on the last card (the one you know).

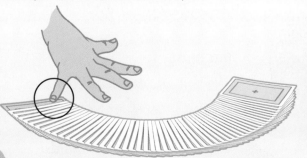

3. Spread the cards out with your fingers. Keep the card you know near the edge. Remember its position before removing your finger.

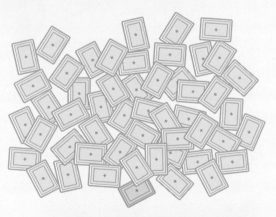

Magic Secrets

This method of staying one move ahead is called the one-ahead principle.

I think this is... the two of spades!

4. Hover your hands over the cards, then press a finger on one. Pretend to work out what it is—and name the card you memorized.

5. Pick up the card, look at it and smile as if you were right. Set it aside, face down.

6. Choose another, and name the card you just looked at.

This one is... the jack of hearts!

7. Pick it up, look pleased and set it on the first.

Concentrate hard as you "sense" each card.

8. Pretend to sense a final card. Go for the card you knew from the start—but say the name of the card you chose last time.

9. Look at the card, then pick up the other two and hide all three in your hand. Remind your friend which you named—then show that you were right!

This one is the three of... diamonds!

And here they are—the two of spades, jack of hearts, and three of diamonds!

Useful Magic Words

ace
A card with just one heart, diamond, spade, or club.

cutting
Picking up the top section of a pack of cards and moving it underneath the pack.

dealing
Taking cards from the pack one by one and laying them in a pile or line.

deck
Another word for a pack of playing cards.

joker
A card that has a jester or clown on it. Jokers are used in some card games, or to replace lost cards.

riffle shuffle
A neat way of shuffling cards on the table instead of in your hands.

shuffling
Mixing a pack of cards in your hands. Usually you need to shuffle a pack a few times before it is properly mixed.

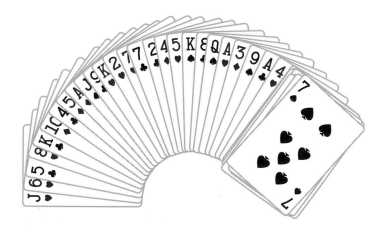

sleight of hand (say "slight")
The skill of secretly moving
or swapping cards to make
a trick work. Sleight of hand
moves are often called
sleights for short and may
take years to learn.

suit
One of the four sets of cards
in a pack. There are two red
suits (hearts and diamonds)
and two black suits (clubs and
spades). Practice recognizing
each suit before you begin
performing magic tricks.

Magic Web Sites

To learn more about card magic and try extra
card tricks, visit these helpful web sites.

www.kidzone.ws/magic

www.amazingkidsmagic.com/free-card-magic-tricks.html

**www.magic.about.com/od/Card-Magic-Tricks/
Card-Magic-Tricks.htm**

Index